VERTICAL POETRY:

RECENT POEMS

BY

ROBERTO JUARROZ

Edited and

Translated By

Mary Crow

White Pine Press

ACKNOWLEDGMENTS: Some of the poems in this book have previously been published by the following magazines: *Agni, Another Chicago Magazine* (ACM), *Artful Dodge, The Connecticut Poetry Review, Exquisite Corpse, Graham House Review, Mid-American Review, Review: Latin American Art and Literature, The Literary Review, Pequod, Ploughshares, Rolling Stock, Sonora Review,* and *Quarterly West.*

TRANSLATOR'S NOTE: I would like to thank both Roberto Juarroz and Laura Cerrato for their many kindnesses, for their great help in reviewing my manuscript, and for their continued encouragement. I would also like to thank Colorado State University for research funding that allowed me to travel to Argentina to work on this project. Finally, I would like to thank Patsy Boyer, my colleague at Colorado State, for her aid in revising the manuscript and for her continuing support.

Cover Design: Based on a detail of a quilt by Nancy Crow entitled "Ratrace"

White Pine Press
76 Center Street
Fredonia, NY 14063

TABLE OF CONTENTS

Introduction

Spanish/English

INTRODUCTION

"Each poem of Roberto Juarroz is a surprising verbal crystalization: language reduced to a drop of light," in the words of the distinguished Mexican poet Octavio Paz, winner in 1990 of the Nobel Prize for Literature. Paz considers Juarroz " a great poet of absolute instants." In Juarroz's poems we do not find the horizontal sweep, the painterly perspectives of much contemporary poetry; instead, we encounter the vertical depths of language, the inward wells.

Born in Coronel Dorrego near Buenos Aires in 1925, Juarroz has published eleven volumes of poetry, each volume entitled *Vertical Poetry*, and is finishing a twelfth volume. To distinguish his books from each other, Juarroz numbers them. Within each book, the poems are also numbered, with no titles to stop the flow as they tumble one after the other, developing Juarroz's themes by moving forward a little, then backwards, then forward again, zigzagging. Their concerns are not so much the personal lives of individuals, particular places and times, but the vertical reaches of thought, the paradoxes of language, the limits of consciousness, the parenthesis of death.

In Juarroz's body of work, there are no phases of development or periods of experimentation with various styles and techniques. His poetry, from his first book, *First Vertical Poetry*, published in 1958, to his most recent, *Eleventh Vertical Poetry*, published in 1988, employs the same style and the same form, the themes continuing from book to book where they are looked at by the poet/speaker, described, turned over and re-examined, re-named, looked at again, re-described in the relentless interplay of Juarroz's attempt to fix the mobility of life and ideas. Among Juarroz's main concerns are words and naming, objectivity and subjectivity, freedom, man and otherness, love, sight and insight, solitude and loneliness, dream and reality, silence and music, naming and nature/power, and the process of thought.

The typical Juarroz poem is aphoristic, taking the form of a riddle or syllogism, mixing abstraction with image ("Life sketches a tree"). His work has been compared to Heraclitus' aphoristic philosophical writings. Guillermo Sucre in *La máscara, la transparencia: ensayos sobre poesía hispanoaméricana (Mask, Transparency: Essays on Spanish-American Poetry)*, speaks of Juarroz's poems as a "sum of fragments or a succession of enigmatic aphorisms" and he adds that Juarroz's "verbal system" is based on "the necessary paradox."

Juarroz's vision, then, is not horizontal, does not follow the land/ landscape or history, least of all that bit of history, a particular life. It attempts instead a view of the depths, and heights, presented so playfully that we are prevented from feeling that we are being addressed by a self-proclaimed prophet. Moreover, while sometimes the subject is God or the nature of the universe, the focus is also at times on something small, a leaf or a butterfly, and frequently the voice that speaks to us is bemused or quizzical, even when it tells us, "We have no other remedy, then, /but to be paradise."

While it is difficult to think of any English language poets with whom to compare Juarroz, he does belong to a tradition in Argentina. His special predecessor was the late Anotonio Porchia (1886-1969) whose books also were all published under only one title, *Voces (Voices)*, and who belonged to the Surrealist circle that was writing and issuing manifestoes in Buenos Aires starting in the late 1920s and continuing through the 1940s and 1950s under the leadership of the poet Aldo Pellegrini (1903-1973). Juarroz has successors as well, notably Guillermo Boido, with whom Juarroz co-authored *Poesía y creación: Diálogos (Poetry and Creation: Dialogues)*. Internationally, Juarroz might be compared to Vasko Popa, the Yugoslavian poet who has written poems also based on repetitive structures, especially the game form.

Also a critic, Roberto Juarroz has published, besides the just mentioned *Poesía y creación: Diálogos con Guillermo Boido*, 1980, *Poesía, literatura, y hermenéutica: conversaciones (Poetry,*

Literature, and Hermeneutics: Conversations, 1987, with Teresita
Saguí), and *Poesía y realidad* (*Poetry and Reality*, 1987).

His entire body of poetry has been translated into French,
and part of his work has been translated into German, Italian,
Portuguese, Greek, Danish, Dutch, Romanian, Hindu, Arabic as
well as English. In 1977, Kayak Books published *Vertical Poetry*,
translated by W.S. Merwin who has also translated selected
poems of Antonio Porchia. In 1987, North Point Press published
a large selection of Merwin's translations of Juarroz's poems from
his first through his seventh volumes (with a few later poems
included) under the title *Vertical Poetry*. The present book
includes work from the eighth through the eleventh volumes,
books published between 1984 and 1988, plus two more recent
unpublished poems.

Roberto Juarroz is a specialist in Library Science and
Information Sciences. He studied at the University of Buenos
Aires and the Sorbonne. Since he completed his studies, he has
worked as a consultant in Library Science for UNESCO and OEA
in Guatemala, Bolivia, Chile, Ecuador, Colombia, Brazil, Costa
Rica, Honduras, Nicaragua, Venezuela, Cuba, France, Belgium,
Denmark, and other countries, and has spoken at many interna-
tional congresses. He served as Vice President of the Latin
American Association of Schools of Library Science and is an
expert in documentary terminology. He has taught as distin-
guished professor in Costa Rica, Colombia, and Bolivia. He
currently teaches at the University of Buenos Aires and lives near
the city with his wife, Laura Cerrato, also a poet, critic, and
professor.

Mary Crow
Fort Collins, Colorado

Vertical Poetry:
Recent Poems

Part I

(from *Eighth
Vertical Poetry*,
1984)

Octava.1

¿Dónde está la sombra
de un objeto apoyado contra la pared?
¿Dónde está la imagen
de un espejo apoyado contra la noche?
¿Dónde está la vida
de una criatura apoyada contra sí misma?
¿Dónde está el imperio
de un hombre apoyado contra la muerte?
¿Dónde está la luz
de un dios apoyado contra la nada?

Tal vez en esos espacios sin espacio
esté lo que buscamos.

Eighth.1

Where's the shadow of an object
propped against the wall?
Where's the image of a mirror
propped against the night?
Where's the life of a being
propped against itself?
Where's the kingdom of a man
propped against death?
Where's the light of a god
propped against nothingness?

Perhaps what we are searching for
exists in that space without space.

Octava.2

También las palabras caen al suelo,
como pájaros repentinamente enloquecidos
por sus propios movimientos,
como objetos que pierden de pronto su equilibrio,
como hombres que tropiezan sin que existan obstáculos,
como muñecos enajenados por su rigidez.

Entonces, desde el suelo,
las proprias palabras construyen una escala,
para ascender de nuevo al discurso del hombre,
a su balbuceo
o a su frase final.

Pero hay algunas que permanecen caídas.
Y a veces uno las encuentra
en un casi larvado mimetismo,
como si supiesen que alguien va a ir a recogerlas
para construir con ellas un nuevo lenguaje,
un lenguaje hecho solamente con palabras caídas.

Eighth.2

Words too fall to the ground,
like birds suddenly driven crazy
by their own movements,
like objects that suddenly lose their balance,
like men who stumble even when there's no obstacle,
like dolls estranged by their own rigidity.

Then, the words themselves build a stairway
from the ground,
to climb up to human discourse,
to its stutter
or final sentence.

But some words remain forever fallen.
And sometimes we find such words
in an almost larval mimesis,
as if they knew someone were going to come
gather them up and build a new language,
a language made up entirely of fallen words.

Octava.9

Tengo un pájaro negro
para que vuele de noche.
Y para que vuele de día
tengo un pájaro vacío.

Pero he descubierto
que ambos se han puesto de acuerdo
para ocupar el mismo nido,
la misma soledad.

Por eso, a veces,
suelo quitarles ese nido,
para ver qué hacen
cuando les falta el retorno.

Y así he aprendido
un increible dibujo:
el vuelo sin condiciones
en lo absolutamente abierto.

(Para Laura, todavía)

Eighth.9

I have a black bird
so I can fly at night.
And so I can fly by day
I have an empty bird.

But I have discovered
they have agreed
to live in the same nest,
the same solitude.

That's why, sometimes,
I take away their nest,
to see what they'll do
when they can't come home again.

And so I've come
to understand an incredible design:
totally free flight
in absolute openness.

(For Laura, still)

Octava.20

Barrer de vez en cuando el pensamiento
hasta dejarlo como un patio vacío,
para que allí dibujen sus piruetas
los acróbatas del olvido.

Y aunque las precoces hormigas del recuerdo
trabajen por debajo,
surgirá de pronto un pensamiento diferente,
un pensamiento quizá frágil, tal vez roto,
pero con otra sustancia entretejida.

Y no importará de dónde venga.
El pensar debe ser siempre otra cosa,
por ejemplo la imagen de una imagen sin sombra
en un patio vacío.

Eighth.20

To sweep thought from time to time
until you leave it like an empty patio,
so that the acrobats of forgetfulness
can sketch their pirouettes there.

And even though memory's precocious ants
keep working down below,
a new thought will soon emerge,
a thought maybe fragile, broken perhaps,
but woven of another substance.

And it won't matter where the thought comes from.
Thought should always be something different,
for example the image of an image
without a shadow in an empty patio.

Octava.50

Cada hombre tiene dos nombres:
uno entero y otro roto.

El nombre entero
reúne sus partículas unánimes,
su transitoria consistencia,
el grado de fusíon de su sombra y su cuerpo,
su aleatoria constancia de ser uno y no otro,
su reconocimiento de los huecos del mundo,
la desbordada suma
de su vida y su muerte.
Y hasta el amor, a veces.

El nombre roto, en cambio,
recoge los fragmentos del hombre,
aquello a que se alude con sigilo,
los restos de las cuentas perdidas,
los asombros que caen,
las astillas del espejo interior,
la locura de convocar los límites,
el trabalenguas del fracaso.
Y hasta el amor, a veces.

Pero entre ambos nombres se despliega
una archa franja sin premura,
una tierra de nadie de los nombres,
una zona ya ni rota ni entera,
donde emerge,
como un signo sin trazo,
la presencia radical de lo anónimo.

Y es allí donde crece,
reelaborando lo imposible,
la última nominación,
la más precisa,
la que no necesita ni siquiera
la distancia del nombre.

Eighth.50

Every man has two names:
one whole and one broken.

The whole name
joins its unanimous particles,
its fleeting consistency,
degree of fusion between shadow and body,
constant randomness of being one and not another,
recognition of the gaps in the world,
overflowing sum
of life and death.
And even love, sometimes.

On the other hand, the broken name
gathers together man's fragments
whatever we refer to in secret,
subtractions from our lost accounts,
surprises that happen,
splinters of our inner mirror,
craziness of touching the limits,
tongue twisters of failure.
And even love, sometimes.

But between the two names
a wide fringe unfurls without haste,
a no man's land of names,
a zone neither broken nor whole,
where the radical presence of the anonymous
emerges,
like a sign without shape.

And it is there
where the final naming grows,
most precise,
reelaborating the impossible,
what doesn't need
even the distance of the name.

Octava.60

¿Qué se esconde detrás de los colores?
¿Será la ausencia del color y la luz?
¿Será tal vez otro color desconocido?
¿O será simplemente
un comienzo que ignoramos de las cosas?

Porque todo color disimula algo,
lo reviste de un juego para el ojo,
de una canción que no se canta,
de un consuelo en las sombras.

Pero si existe otro color de fondo,
¿existirá también un ojo que lo vea?
¿O detrás de los colores no hay nada más que un ojo
que nos mira a través de ellos?

Eighth.60

What's hidden behind colors?
Can it be the absence of color and light?
Can it be perhaps another unknown color?
Or can it simply be
a beginning of things we don't know?

Because every color hides something,
and dresses it up in a outfit for the eye,
in a song that isn't sung,
in a consolation in the darkness.

But if another color exists in the background,
will an eye also exist to see it?
Or behind the colors is there nothing but an eye
that looks at us through them?

Octava.72

¿Qué borrar primero:
la sombra o el cuerpo,
la palabra escrita ayer
o la palabra escrita hoy,
el día oscuro
o el día claro?

Hay que encontrar un orden.
El aprendizaje de borrar el mundo
nos ayudará luego a borrarnos.

Eighth.72

Which to erase first:
shadow or body,
the word written yesterday
or the word written today,
the cloudy day
or the clear day?

One has to find an order.
Learning to erase the world
will soon help us to erase ourselves.

Octava.76

Alguien o su substituto
nos espera a la vuelta de la esquina,
aunque allí no haya nadie
y aunque ni siquiera haya esquina.

Alguien o su reemplazante
nos espera en cada cosa,
como si en cada una hubiese
una historia que nos fuera a ser contada.

Alguien o su doble
nos espera en cada gesto o movimiento que
                                    [repetimos,
con el semblante de un viejo conocido
que viniese a nuestro encuentro.

No se trata del mismo o de lo mismo,
ya sea titular o suplente,
ni se trata tampoco
de darle en cada caso un nombre.

La disfunción es otra:
no sabemos todavía quién o qué nos espera adentro.
Y entonces no sabemos actuar
como alguien que es de veras esperado.

Por otra parte,
ya todo nos resulta obstinadamente insistente,
un paso más acá de la distancia
que requiere la espera.

Eighth.76

Someone or his substitute
waits for us just around the corner,
even though there's no one there
and though there isn't even a corner.

Someone or his replacement
waits for us in each thing,
as if in each thing there were
a story waiting to be told to us.

Someone or his double
waits for us in each gesture or movement we repeat,
with the face of an old friend
who came out to meet us.

This has nothing to do with the same or sameness,
either natural or exceptional,
nothing to do either, in any case,
with giving things a name.

Disfunction is different.
We don't know yet who or what waits for us inside.
And so we don't know how to act
like someone who is truly expected.

On the other hand,
everything now seems obstinately insistent to us,
one step this side of the distance
waiting requires.

Octava.83

La escritura infecta aquí el paisaje.
Hay más letras que hojas.
La palabra del hombre
se ha convertido en floración parásita.

La escritura cubre así otra escritura
y no deja mirar hacia otro lado,
hacia la fiesta pura de leer en el fondo
el secreto alfabeto que no se deletrea.

Hay que cavar detrás de la escritura,
hasta encontrar la otra, la cegada.
Ya estamos en los últimos renglones
y no hemos terminado todavía el mensaje.

Eighth.83

Here writing infects the landscape.
There are more letters than leaves.
Man's word has been turned
into parasitical flowers.

Here writing covers up another writing
and doesn't let you look elsewhere,
toward the pure joy of reading deeply
the secret alphabet that can't be spelled out.

You must dig beyond the writing,
until you find the other writing, the blind writing.
We are already on the last lines
and still haven't completed the message.

Vertical Poetry:
Recent Poems

Part II

(From *Ninth
Vertical Poetry*,
1986)

Novena.2

Traer el horizonte a nuestro lado,
desplegarlo en la calle como una bandera,
incendiar con su cuerpo desnudo
el aire, el corazón y los rincones
y cerrar las ventanas para que no desaparezca.

Iniciar entonces su conversión,
hasta ponerlo firmemente de pie,
como un árbol o un amor desvelado.
Y cambiar el horizonte en vertical,
en una fina torre
que nos salve por los menos la mirada,
hacia arriba o abajo.

Ninth.2

To drag the horizon to our side,
to unfurl it in the street like a flag,
to set the air, heart, and corners aflame
with its naked body
and lock the windows so it won't go away.

Then to initiate its conversion,
until it stands firmly on its feet,
like a tree or an unsleeping love.
And to change horizontal into vertical,
into a slender tower
that at least shifts our glance for us,
to up and down.

Novena.3

Celebrar lo que no existe.
¿Hay otro camino para celebrar lo que existe?

Celebrar lo imposible.
¿Hay otro modo de celebrar lo posible?

Celebrar el silencio.
¿Hay otra manera de celebrar la palabra?

Celebrar le soledad.
¿Hay otra vía para celebrar el amor?

Celebrar el revés.
¿Hay otra forma de celebrar el derecho?

Celebrar lo que muere.
¿Hay otra senda para celebrar lo que vive?

El poema es siempre celebración
porque es siempre el extremo
de la intensidad de un pedazo del mundo,
su espalda de fervor restituido,
su puño de desenvarado entusiasmo,
su más justa pronunciación, la más firme,
como si estuviera floreciendo la voz.

El poema es siempre celebración,
aunque en sus bordes se refleje el infierno,
aunque el tiempo se crispe como un órgano herido,
aunque el funambulesco histrión que empuja las
[palabras
desbande sus volteretas y sus guiños.

Nada puede ocultar a lo infinito.
Su gesto es más amplio que la historia,
su paso es más largo que la vida.

24

Ninth.3

Celebrating what doesn't exist.
Is there another road to celebrating what exists?

Celebrating the impossible.
Is there another path for celebrating the possible?

Celebrating silence.
Is there another fashion for celebrating the word?

Celebrating solitude.
Is there another way to celebrate love?

Celebrating the upside down.
Is there another form of celebrating the right side up?

Celebrating what dies.
Is there another path for celebrating what lives?

The poem is always celebration
because it is always the extreme intensity
of a chunk of the world,
its backbone of renewed fervor,
its punch of unbenumbed enthusiasm,
its most perfect and firmest pronunciation,
as if the voice were in bloom.

The poem is always celebration
even though hell is reflected on its edges,
even though time twitches like a wounded organ,
even though a tight-rope performer
who pushes words
forgets his somersaults and his winks.
Nothing can hide the infinite.
Its gesture is broader than history,
its step longer than life.

Novena.5

Morir, pero lejos.
No aquí,
donde todo es una aviesa
conspiración de la vida,
hasta las otras muertes.

Morir lejos.
No aquí,
donde morir es ya una traición,
más traición que en otra parte.

Morir lejos.
No aquí,
donde le soledad descansa a ratos
como si fuera un animal tendido,
olvidando su espuela de locura.

Morir lejos.
No aquí,
donde cada uno se duerme
siempre en el mismo sitio,
aunque despierte siempre en otro.

Morir lejos.
No aquí.
Morir donde nadie nos espere,
donde haya lugar para morir.

(para Jorge Luis Borges)

Ninth.5

To die, but far away.
Not here,
where everything is crooked,
conspiracy of life,
including other deaths.

To die far away.
Not here,
where dying is already a betrayal,
a greater betrayal than elsewhere.

To die far away.
Not here,
where solitude rests every once in a while
as if it were an animal stretched out,
forgetting its spur of craziness.

To die far away.
Not here,
where every one of us sleeps
always in the same place,
even though we always wake somewhere else.

To die far away.
Not here.
To die where no one waits for us,
where there is a place to die.

(For Jorge Luis Borges)

Novena.11

Cada cosa es un mensaje,
un pulso que se muestra,
una escotilla en el vacío.

Pero entre los mensajes de las cosas
se van dibujando otros mensajes,
allí en el intervalo,
entre una cosa y otra,
conformados por ellas y sin ellas,
como si lo que está
decidiera sin querer el estar
de aquello que no está.

Buscar esos mensajes intermedios,
la forma que se forma entre las formas,
es completar el código.
O tal vez descubrirlo.

Buscar la rosa
que queda entre las rosas.

Y aunque no sean rosas.

Ninth.11

Each thing is a message,
a pulse that reveals itself,
a trap door in the emptiness.

But between the messages of things
other messages get sketched,
there in the interval,
between one thing and another,
shaped by things or their absence,
as if what is
should decide involuntarily the being
of what isn't.

To find those intermediary messages,
the form that is formed among the forms,
is to complete the code.
Or perhaps to discover it.

To find the rose
that remains among the roses.

Even though they aren't roses.

Novena.13

Las obsesiones del lenguaje,
como todas las obsesiones,
nos visitan de noche.
A veces, despiertos,
pero casi siempre dormidos.

Entonces desaprendemos
lo que parece que sabemos
e inauguramos
lo que parece que ignoramos.

Por eso
los poemas se escriben de noche,
aunque a veces se disfracen de luz.
O si se escriben de día,
convierten el día en noche.

Ninth.13

Obsessions with language,
like all obsessions,
visit us at night.
Sometimes when we are awake,
but almost always when we are asleep.

Then we un-learn
what we thought we knew
and we begin to learn
what we thought we didn't know.

That's why poems are written at night,
though sometimes they disguise
themselves in light.
Or if they are written by day
they turn day into night.

Novena.34

Depertar es siempre
una difícil emergencia:
reencender la lucidez
como quien recomienza el mundo.

Por eso nos quedamos
en los estados intermedios.
El hombre no es una criatura despierta:
desconoce lo abierto.

Llamas que se consumen a medias,
párpados que se olvidan del ojo,
jardines paralizados en la noche,
huecos de la intemperie acorralada.

Los caminos se aglomeran en vano:
despertar es borrar los caminos.

Ninth.34

Waking is always
a difficult emergency:
a re-kindling of lucidity
like one who starts the world over again.

That's why we stay
in intermediate states.
Man isn't a creature awake:
He doesn't know openness.

Flames that are half consumed,
eyelids that forget the eye,
gardens paralyzed at night,
gaps besieged by bad weather.

Roads converge in vain:
waking up is erasing the roads.

Novena.39

La nieve ha convertido al mundo en cementerio.
Pero el mundo ya era un cementerio
y la nieve sólo ha venido a publicarlo.

La nieve sólo ha venido a señalar,
con su delgado dedo sin articulaciones,
al verdadero y escandaloso protagonista.

La nieve es un ángel caído,
un ángel que ha perdido la paciencia.

Ninth.39

Snow has turned the world into a cemetery.
But the world already was a cemetery
and the snow has only come to announce it.

The snow has only come to point,
with its slender jointless finger,
at the truly outrageous protagonist.

The snow is a fallen angel,
an angel who has lost patience.

Novena.41

Sacudir el cuerpo como lo haría un animal,
pero quitándose de encima mucho más que el animal:
el polvo que deja el pensamiento,
las rigideces que enrolan a la muerte,
las manchas del amor y de las illuvias sucias
que caen de las cornisas
y también de un cielo turbio, envenenado.

Y quitarse de encima los andrajos del tiempo,
las contraseñas de los cuartos grises,
los moretones de la dicha,
los restos pegajosos del banquete,
las macabras serpentinas del dolor.

Y en un día de calculados estremecimientos
quitarse uno de encima hasta su sombra,
hasta eso que llamamos uno mismo,
hasta esos roces que llamamos los otros.

Y otro día sacudirse de encima
la eternidad desfigurada de la vida,
como si fuera otra capa de polvo.

Ninth.41

Shaking the body as an animal does,
but shaking off more than the animal:
the dust that thinking leaves,
the rigidities that enlist death,
stains of love and of dirty rains
that fall from the cornices
and also from a turbid and poisoned sky.

And getting rid of the tatters of time,
passwords of the gray rooms,
bruises of joy,
sticky leftovers from the banquet,
macabre streamers of pain.

And in one day of calculated shudders
to get rid of our own shadow,
even what we call the self,
even those rubbings we call others.

And the next day shaking off
of life's disfigured eternity from on top of ourselves,
as if it were another layer of dust.

Novena.48

Para la música oculta en la espuma
debe haber cierto oído de caracol no asplastado
o por lo menos algún tímpano dispuesto
para captar otros sonidos que no sean
las rudas cacofonías de los hombres.

El sonido del silencio, por ejemplo,
o el sonido que recubre como sal toda escritura
o aquél cuyas puertas sólo abren ciertas músicas,
ya que toda la música
no es más que el umbral de otro sonido.

Y aunque carezcamos del órgano apropiado,
como también de otros sentidos
para aprehender las ondas sueltas de la vida,
hay sin embargo en nosotros
un minúsculo extremo de algo,
una axial limadura de luz,
una punta quebrada,
que sin saberlo forma parte también de ese sonido.

Partículas de todo caen sobre nosotros,
partículas extraviadas, partículas previstas,
pero también nosotros caemos sobre todo
y a veces nos fundimos con ese último sonido
como con la vena transparente
de otro viento que pasa.

Ninth.48

For the music hidden in the foam
there ought to be an uncrushed shell's ear
or at least some waiting drum
to capture other sounds that aren't
the rough cacophonies of men.

The sound of silence, for example,
or the sound that, like salt, coats all writing
or that sound whose doors are opened only by certain music,
since all music
is only the threshold of other sound.

And even if we lack the appropriate organ,
and all the other senses too,
to apprehend the unleashed waves of life,
there is nonetheless in us
a miniscule bit of something,
axial filings of light,
a broken point,
that, without our knowing, also forms part of that sound.

Particles of everything fall on us,
lost particles, expected particles,
but we too fall on everything
and sometimes we blend with that last sound
as with the transparent vein
of another wind that passes.

Vertical Poetry:
Recent Poems

Part III

(from *Tenth
Vertical Poetry*,
1986)

Décima.3

En todos los mundos
hay imágenes flotantes,
íconos vagabundos
cuyo destino es ir a la deriva,
figuras que inquietan a los seres fijos
y a las cosas atadas.

Pero hay además mundos
hechos solamente de imágenes,
sin anclajes ni puertos,
íntegramente nómades,
destellos sín raíz,
fulguración en fuga.

Toda imagen tiende espontáneamente
a descartar su fuente
y valerse a sí misma.
Y esos mundos de imágenes flotantes
intentan también prescindir de los otros
en busca de un espacio más libre.

Porque más allá de la pesadez de los cuerpos,
sólo las imágenes son libres.
Por lo tanto debe el hombre
convertirse en imagen.
O dejar que su imagen se vaya libremente
y aprender a quedarse sin imagen.

Tenth.3

In every world
there are floating images,
vagabond icons
whose destiny is to float adrift,
figures disquieting to fixed beings
and to everything tied-down.

But there are also worlds
made only of images,
without anchorage or ports,
entirely nomadic,
rootless glimmerings,
fleeting flashes.

Every image tends to stretch out spontaneously,
discard its source
and stand on its own.
And those worlds of floating images
also try to do without the others
in search of a freer space.

Because beyond the weight of bodies,
only images are free.
Therefore man ought
to turn into image.
Or let his image drift freely
and learn to exist with no image.

Décima.9

Todo poema es una vacilación de la historia.
Cubrir la historia con poemas
equivale a que sus capas se desplacen
más allá de las acciones de los hombres.

El poema también es una acción,
un movimiento del terreno que pisamos,
pero en sentido inverso,
hacia donde casi todo se abstiene.

Allí donde al final va casi todo,
pero en triste y obligado cortejo,
invocando los huesos de la historia,
sus cuaresmales zonas superpuestas.

El poema salta afuera de la historia
como animal de caza
que trastornando el orden de esas capas
pone otra capa encima: lo infinito.

Y entonces el animal de caza
descarta la presa siempre fósil de la historia
y repliega también su propia garra,
para correr por fin al aire libre.

(para Fernand Verhesen)

Tenth.9

Every poem is a hesitation of history.
Covering history with poems
is like displacing its layers
beyond the actions of men.

The poem also is an act,
a movement of the earth we tread,
but in the reverse direction,
toward where everything is absent.

There, where almost everything goes in the end,
but in a sad and forced procession,
invoking the bones of history,
with its lenten, overlaid zones.

The poem leaps out of history
like a hunted animal
that overturns those layers,
and puts another layer on top: the infinite.

And then the hunted animal
discards its fossilized prey of history
and also sheathes its claws,
running at last in the free air.

(For Fernand Verhesen)

Décima.12

Toda palabra debe ser soñada
antes de llegar al poema.

Salir del espectáculo y el mercado verbal,
saltar hacia atrás del decorado
y acceder a esa zona oculta
donde el aire es tan fino
que en sus micropartículas extremas
ya no hay diferencia entre la luz y la sombra.

Y a la luz de esa no luz
o más o menos u otra cosa que luz,
hallar el hilo más tenso de la preforma del lenguaje,
ahorcarse con él como un animal mínimo y suicida
y renacer como renace lo sagrado
antes y después de los dioses.

Podrá entonces la palabra
bautizarse de nuevo en el poema,
aunque su sueño de palabra ya no termine nunca
y la siga como un traje de bodas
que se adhirió para siempre al cuerpo de la novia
después de la nupcial liturgia.

Tenth.12

Every word ought to be dreamed
before becoming poem.

To emerge from the show and the word market,
to leap behind the stage setting
and to accede to that secret zone
where the air is so rare
that in its tiniest microparticles
there's no longer any difference between light and shadow.

And by the light of that non-light
or more or less light, or something other than light,
to find the tensest thread of the pre-form of language,
with which to hang yourself like a minimal suicidal animal
and be reborn as the sacred is reborn
before and after the gods.

Then the word
could be rebaptized in the poem,
even though its word-dream never ends
and follows it like a wedding gown
clinging forever to the bride's body
after the wedding ceremony.

Décima.13

Sólo la música
puede ocupar el lugar del pensamiento.
O su nolugar,
su autoespacio vacío
su vacío lleno.

El pensamiento es otra música.

Y sólo el pensamiento
puede ocupar a su vez el lugar de la música
e infiltrarse como ella
en el extremo más distante de lo que existe,
como un casi animal tan consecuentemente fino
que puede entonces llegar hasta ese punto
donde el ser deja de ser el ser
para ser algo más que el ser.

Tenth.13

Only music
can take the place of thought.
Or its non-place,
its empty self-space
its full emptiness.

Thought is a different music.

And only thought
can, in its turn, take the place of music
and like it infiltrate the extreme,
the furthest point of what exists,
like an almost animal as a consequence so fine
it can therefore get to that point
where being stops being being
to become something more than being.

Décima.19

La barbarie de la muerte,
la rústica pantomoma de la muerte
y su cruel y vulgar inhumanidad,
no hacen juego con el pensamiento.

Tal vez el amor o el dolor
puedan pactar con ella
y quizá también la música o el sueño,
pero el pensamiento es una bandera
plantada en otra parte,
como lo es además la poesía.

Ambos enrolan en su índole abierta
las antinomias de la muerte.
Sin embargo,
una cosa es sacar rostros de la nada
y otra cosa es borrarlos.
Lo mismo con testigos o sin ellos.

Precisamente,
la poesía y el pensar
son lo más opuesto a la muerte
porque son sus testigos más fieles.

Tenth.19

The barbarity of death,
the rustic pantomime of death
and its cruel and vulgar inhumanity,
don't go with thought.

Perhaps love or pain
can make a pact with death
and maybe also music or dreams,
but thought is a flag
planted somewhere else,
as poetry also is.

Both wrap up the antimonies of death
in their own nature.
Nonetheless,
it's one thing to draw faces out of nothing
and another to erase them.
It's the same whether there are witnesses or not.

Poetry and thought
are precisely
the most opposed to death
because they are its most faithful witnesses.

Décima.20

Si esto es uno
¿qué será dos?

No es tan sólo uno más uno.
A veces es dos
y no deja de ser uno
Como a veces uno
no deja tampoco de ser dos.

Las cuentas de la realidad no son claras
o por lo menos no lo es
nuestra lectura de sus resultados.
Se nos escapa así
lo que hay entre uno y uno,
se nos escapa lo que hay
simplemente adentro de uno,
se nos escapa
lo que hay en menos uno,
se nos escapa el cero
que circunvala o acompaña siempre
a uno y a dos.

La rosa, ¿es una?
El amor, ¿es dos?
El poema, ¿es ninguno?

Tenth.20

If this is one,
what would two be?

It's not just one plus one.
Sometimes it's two
while it's still one.
Just as one also
sometimes doesn't stop being two.

Accounts of reality aren't clear
or at least not our reading
of the results.
So what there is between one and one
escapes us,
what there is simply inside of one
escapes us,
what there is in minus one
escapes us,
the zero escapes us
that always bypasses or accompanies
a one and a two.

The rose—is it one?
Love—is it two?
The poem—is it either?

Décima.28

Eras el portador de la aventura,
el huésped de lo insólito,
titular de los trajines del milagro,
depositario de las rúbricas del viento,
capitán del azul inesperado,
reinventor general de lo existente.

No importa que las costras de la vida
sometieran tu heráldico penacho.
No importa que tu enorme expectativa
se hundiera en los sarcófagos bruñidos.
No importa que tus manos siempre abiertas
te las hayan cerrado con usuras.
No importa que tus sueños para todos
se volvieran un sueño para nadie.

Basta sencillamente que hayas sido
lo que alguna vez fuiste:
un hueco de tos joven
en la cueva envejecida del mundo.

(a Oscar)

Tenth.28

You were the bearer of adventure,
the host of the unusual,
holder of miracle's intricacy,
deposit of the wind's rubrics,
captain of the unexpected blue,
overall re-inventor of all that exists.

It doesn't matter that the scabs of life
vanquished your heraldic crests.
It doesn't matter that your enormous hope
drowned in the burnished sarcophagi.
It doesn't matter that your always open hands
have been closed with usury.
It doesn't matter that your dreams for everyone
have become no one's dream.

It's enough simply that you have been
what you once were:
a hollow of youthful cough
in the old cave of the world.

(To Oscar)

Décima.32

Marcó ciertas palabras para siempre
como espigas de hueso despierto
en el trigo de sangre y reverbero del lenguaje,
pero no las marcó con lápiz ni con tiza
sino cone ese tilde del silencio
que sube desde adentro de la tierra
y se mezcla con la sal de la música
en los cuerpos quemantes y quemados.

Marcó ciertas palabras para siempre
y ellas lo marcaron para siempre,
porque había que llevar otra vez al poema
la hiel y los claveles que enlazan los caminos
y también los más tercos ademanes
del amor y del odio,
del coraje y el duelo,
esos focos de resurrección sin muerte.

Marcó ciertas palabras.
Las cantó para todos.
Las enancó en el lomo
del color y la música.
Nos entibió con ellas
la mano en el arado
que cada cual trabaja.
Nos dibujó de nuevo
este mundo y los otros.
Nos mostró que es posible
ser hombre y ser destino.

Marcó ciertas palabras para siempre.
¿Qué más pedirle a un hombre
que además es un duende?
¿Qué más pedirle a un hombre
que marcha hacia la muerte?
¿Qué más pedirle a un hombre
que abrió el sol y la luz
como un limón maduro?

Tenth.32

He marked certain words forever,
like grain-spikes of wakened bone
in the wheat of blood and reverberation of language,
yet he didn't mark them with pencil or chalk
but with that tick of silence
that mounts from within the earth
and is mixed with the salt of music
in bodies burned and burning.

He marked certain words forever
and they marked him forever,
because he had to take to the poem again
the gall and carnations that connect the paths
and even the most stubborn gestures
of love and hate,
courage and grief,
those focuses of resurrection without death.

He marked certain words.
He sang them for everyone.
He mounted them on the back
of color and music.
With words he warmed
our hands on the plough
everyone pushes.
Again he sketched for us
this world and other worlds.
He showed us it's possible
to be man and destiny.

He marked certain words forever.
What more can you ask of a man
who was also a magician?
What more can you ask of a man
who marches toward death?
What more can you ask of a man
who split the sun and light open
like a ripe lemon?

Marcó ciertas palabras.
Creyó ciertas palabras.
Creó ciertas palabras.
No las olvidaremos.
No olvidar es la forma
de proseguir marcando para siempre
las palabras y el mundo.

(a Federico García Lorca)

He marked certain words.
He believed certain words.
He created certain words.
We will not forget them.
Not to forget is the way
to go on marking forever
words and world.

(To Federico García Lorca)

Décima.36

Cuando cesan todos los brindis
suele quedar un silencio en el silencio
o una media voz en la voz
que alude al otro lado de las cosas.

Cuando termina el brindis por el ser
debe empezar el brindis por el no ser.
La diferencia es poca,
sólo tal vez una escueta vibración en el aire.

O quizá cierto gusto tímido en el vino.
Pero la copa y la mano son las mismas.

Tenth.36

When all the toasts come to an end
there's usually a silence in the silence
or a half voice in the voice
that alludes to the other side of things.

When the toast for being ends,
the toast for not being ought to begin.
The difference is slight,
except perhaps for a sparse vibration in the air.

Or maybe a certain timid taste in the wine.
But the glass and the hand are the same.

Décima.42

La locura de no estar loco,
de rechazar con el brazo estirado
las zonas interiores
donde aguarda la ciénaga,
hace pisar a veces
los pies abandonados.

No estar loco,
el algunos momentos,
se parece demasiado a la locura.
Excesiva, insoportable intensidad,
defendiéndose a la vez de las greñas flotantes
y del cabello intolerablemente liso.

Es preciso, cada tanto,
descansar de no estar loco.

Tenth.42

The craziness of not being crazy,
of repulsing with the extended arm
the interior zones
where the swamp waits,
making abandoned feet
touch ground sometimes.

Not being crazy
sometimes
resembles craziness too much.
Excessive, unbearable intensity,
defending itself simultaneously from the floating tangles
and from the intolerably smooth hair.

It's necessary, every so often,
to rest from not being crazy.

Décima.44

Me doy vuelta hacia tu lado,
en el lecho o la vida,
y encuentro que estás hecha de imposible.

Me vuelvo entonces hacia mí
y hallo la misma cosa.

Es por eso
que aunque amemos lo posible,
terminaremos por encerrarlo en una caja,
para que no estorbe más a este imposible
sin el cual no podemos seguir juntos.

(para Laura otra vez, mientras nos acercamos)

Tenth.44

I turn toward your side,
in bed or in life,
and I find that you are impossible.

I turn then toward myself
and I find the same thing.

Therefore
even though we love the possible,
we end by shutting it up in a box,
so that it will no longer get in the way of this impossible
without which we can't go on together.

(For Laura again, while we draw close to each other)

Décima.52

Estamos en fila.
Nadie sabe para qué.
Debe ser para la muerte.
La vida no es cuestión de formar fila.
O tal vez para la historia o sus flacos sucedáneos,
que tampoco tienen mucho que ver con la vida.

Estamos en fila.
Y la fila apenas se mueve.
Algunos tratan de hacer trampa
y adelantarse cuando creen
que nadie los observa.
Otros, en cambio,
tratan de correrse hacia atrás.

No ha habido ninguna orden.
No es tampoco un problema topográfico,
fisiológico o estratégico.
Estamos en fila
como una lineal concentración
de juncos aturdidos.

Y está vedado,
no sabemos por quién,
tirarse a la vera del camino.
Sólo queda escapar alguna noche
y arrojarse como un dios contra las sombras,
corriendo el riesgo de caer en otra fila.

Porque también los dioses,
por lo menos los pocos que quedaban,
han terminado al fin por formar fila.

(para Julián Polito)

Tenth.52

We are in a line.
No one knows why.
It may be for death.
Life isn't a matter of lining up.
Or perhaps it's the line for history or its skinny substitutes,
that also haven't much to do with life.

We are in a line.
And the line barely moves.
Some try to cheat
and move forward when they think
no one is paying attention to them.
Others, on the other hand,
try to move further back.

There hasn't been any kind of order.
But it's not a topographical problem either,
nor physiological or strategic.
We are in a line
like a linear concentration
of bewildered reeds.

And it's forbidden,
we don't know by whom,
to lie down beside the road.
All that's left to do is escape some night
and hurl ourselves like a god against the shadows,
running the risk of falling into another line.

Because also the gods,
at least the remaining few,
have ended up forming a line.

(For Julián Polito)

Décima.57

Los nombres no designan a las cosas:
las envuelven, las sofocan.

Pero las cosas rompen
sus envolturas de palabras
y vuelven a estar ahí, desnudas,
esperando algo más que los nombres.

Sólo puede decirlas
su propia vox de cosa,
la voz que ni ellas ni nosotros sabemos,
en esta neutralidad que apenas habla,
este mutismo enorme donde rompen las olas.

Tenth.57

Names don't designate things:
they enfold them, suffocate them.

But things break
their word wrappings
and, naked, stand there again,
waiting for something more than names.

Only a thing's own voice
can speak of it,
the voice which neither the thing nor we know,
in this neutrality that barely speaks,
this enormous silence where waves break.

Décima.66

Cualquier movimiento mata algo.

Mata el lugar que se abandona,
el gesto, la posición irreptible,
algún anónimo organismo,
una señal, una mirada,
un amor que volvía,
una presencia o su contrario,
la vida siempre de algún otro,
la propria vida sin los otros.

Y estar aquí es moverse,
estar aquí es matar algo.
Hasta los muertos se mueven,
hasta los muertos matan.
Aquí el aire huele a crimen.

Pero el olor viene de más lejos.
Y hasta el olor se mueve.

Tenth.66

Any movement kills something.

It kills the place that is abandoned,
the gesture, the unrepeatable position,
some anonymous organism,
a sign, a glance,
a love that returned,
a presence or its contrary,
the life always of someone else,
one's own life without others.

And being here is moving,
being here is killing something.
Even the dead move,
even the dead kill.
Here the air smells of crime.

But the odor comes from farther away.
And even the odor moves.

Décima.72

El silencio cae de los árboles
como frutos blancos,
madurados bajo la piel de otra luz.

El silencio se va amontonando sobre el suelo
y termina por borrar el camino.
El silencio borra todos los caminos,
como la noche o la nieve.

Desaparecen así el comienzo y el fin,
la partida y la llegada,
que se confunden en una sola mancha.

Bajo el silencio
se igualan todos los extremos.

Tenth.72

Silence falls from the trees
like white fruit,
ripened beneath the skin of another light.

Silence gradually piles up on the ground
and ends erasing the road.
Silence erases all the roads,
as night does, or snow.

That's how beginning and end disappear,
departure and arrival,
that are mixed up in a single stain.

In the silence
all extremes are alike.

Vertical Poetry:
Recent Poems

Part IV

(from *Eleventh
Vertical Poetry*,
1988)

Undécima.I.3

Una escritura que soporte la intemperie,
que se pueda leer bajo el sol o la lluvia,
bajo el grito o la noche,
bajo el tiempo desnudo.

Una escritura que soporte la infinito,
las grietas que se reparten como el polen,
la lectura sin piedad de los dioses,
la lectura iletrada del desierto.

Una escritura que resista
la intemperie total.
Una escritura que se pueda leer
hasta en la muerte.

Eleventh.I.3

A writing that withstands bad weather,
that can be read beneath sun or rain,
beneath howling or night,
beneath the nakedness of time.

A writing that withstands the infinite,
cracks that spread like pollen,
reading without the gods' pity,
the desert's illiterate reading.

A writing that resists
absolute bad weather.
A writing that can be read
even in death.

Undécima.I.10

Soñé un manuscrito
cuyas líneas se borraban una a una.
Soñé también a quienes lo escribían
-uno era yo-
y también se borraban uno a uno.

Al despertar
no quedaba ya nadie.
Y había una única línea,
que también comenzaba a borrarse.
Esa línea decía:
Sólo dios puede salvar de dios.

Eleventh.I.10

I dreamed of a manuscript
whose lines were erased one by one.
I also dreamed of those who wrote it --
I was one of them--
and they too were erased one by one.

When I woke
there was no one left.
And there was only one line,
also beginning to be erased.
This line said:
Only god can save one from god.

Undécima.I.13

Hay que cambiar la locura del mundo.
Para iniciar el trabajo
se puede, por ejemplo,
tomar todos los nombres propios
y escribirlos de nuevo con letras minúsculas,
comenzando por el ser más amado
o la mayor ausencia,
sin olvidar tampoco
el nombre propio de la muerte.

Al empequeñecer progresivamente los nombres,
iremos recobrando el vacío que contienen
y quizá podamos hallar como añadido
el nombre propio de la nada.

Y nombrar a la nada
puede ser precisamente
la fundación que nos falta:
la fundación de una locura
que no necesitemos cambiar.

Eleventh.I.13

The craziness of the world must be changed.
To begin this work,
we could, for example,
take all the proper nouns
and write them again with lower case letters,
beginning with the one you love
or the biggest absence,
without overlooking
the proper noun for death.

By making names progressively smaller,
we will be gradually recovering the emptiness they contain
and perhaps we can find an extra,
the proper name of nothingness.

And to name nothingness
could be precisely
the foundation we lack:
the foundation of a craziness
we won't need to change.

Undécima.I.15

¿Debe la rosa devolver sus pétalos?
¿Debe el hombre devolver sus amores?
¿Debe el bardo devolver su palabra?
¿Debe el mundo devolver sus figuras?

¿Quién prestó todo esto?
Aunque no lo sepamos
quizá nuestra función
es volver a prestarlo,
en una incierta ronda
de préstamos rotativos:
pétalos, amores, palabras, figuras.

Préstamos y no devoluciones,
ya que parece no haber nadie
a quien devolver nada.

Eleventh.I.15

Should the rose return its petals?
Man give back his loves?
The poet give back his word?
The world give back its forms?

Who lent us all those things?
Even though we don't know,
perhaps our role
is to lend it all out again,
in an uncertain round
of circulating loans:
petals, loves, words, forms.

Borrowed and never returned,
since there seems to be no one
to whom we can return anything.

Undécima.II.15

Un zumbido de fondo
acusa la presencia de las cosas.
Necesitamos la palabra y el viento
para poder soportarlo.

Un zumbido de fondo
denuncia la ausencia de las cosas.
Necesitamos inventar otra memoria
para no enloquecer.

Un zumbido de fondo
anuncia que no hay nada
que no pueda existir.
Necesitamos un silencio doblado de silencio
para aceptar que todo existe.

Un zumbido de fondo
subraya el frió de la muerte.
Necesitamos la suma de todos los cantos
y el resumen de todos los amores
para poder aplacar ese zumbido.

O una tarde cualquiera,
sin más condición que su abertura,
vendrá un pájaro a posarse en el aire
como si el aire fuera otra rama.
Y entonces cesarán todos los zumbidos.

Eleventh.II.15

A buzz in the background
acknowledges the presence of things.
We need word and wind
to be able to bear it.

A buzz in the background
reveals the absence of things.
We need to invent another memory
in order not to go crazy.

A buzz in the background
announces there is nothing
that cannot exist.
We need a silence folded into silence
to accept that everything exists.

A buzz in the background
underlines the cold of death.
We need the total of all songs
and the sum of every love
to be able to calm that buzz.

Or some afternoon,
with no quality but its openness,
a bird will come to perch in the air
as if the air were another branch.
And then all buzzing will cease.

Undécima.II.22

Murió mi eternidad y estoy velándola.
¿Muere también la eternidad?
¿De qué manera muere?
¿Y cómo se la vela?
¿Con una sola vida o con más vidas?
¿Con los dos ojos o con uno solo,
para poder quizá velar la vida con el otro?
¿Con la cabeza abajo del sombrero
o arriba del sombrero
o sin sombrero para siempre?

No pudimos acompañarte entonces
a velar tu eternidad.
Pero la velaremos ahora,
la tuya tuya
y también la eternidad que nos dejaste
y que lo mismo debe ser velada.
Por ejemplo, ciertas cosas como ésta:
Me moriré en París con aguacero,
un día del cual tengo ya el recuerdo.
O la otra, que siempre nos desvela:
la llave que va a todas las puertas.

Para eso, seguiremos sin apremio
las huellas imposibles
del sitio aquel que descubriste:
Hay un lugar que yo me sé
en este mundo, nada menos,
adonde nunca llegaremos.
Pero allí, por supuesto sin llegar,
como a nada se llega,
velaremos mejor tu eternidad
Y velaremos además tu tiempo,
aquél que se dio vuelta en tus palabras
como en un libro diferente,
con las tapas adentro y las letras afuera,
de un texto que siempre está esperando,
quizá también en ese espacio
del que después dijiste:

86

Eleventh.II.22

My eternity died and I'm holding its wake.
Does eternity also die?
How does it die?
And does one mourn it?
With a single life or with many lives?
With both eyes or with only one eye,
leaving the other free to mourn over life?
With the head beneath the hat
or above the hat
or hatless forever?

We couldn't be with you then
to hold a wake for your eternity.
But we'll hold a wake for it now,
your yours
and also the eternity you left us
which deserves its own wake as well.
For example, certain things like this:
I will die in Paris when there's a sudden shower,
a day I can already remember.
Or something else that keeps us awake always:
the key that fits every door.

For that, we will go on following freely
the impossible traces
of that place you discovered:
There is a place I know
in this world, no less,
where we will never arrive.
But there, of course, never arriving
the way one arrives at nothingness,
we will hold a wake for your eternity.

And we'll also hold a wake for your time,
the time that took a turn in your words
as in a different book,
with the covers inside and the letters outside,
of a text that is always waiting,
perhaps also in that space
of which you said later:

Mas el lugar que yo me sé
en este mundo, nada menos,
hombreado va con los reversos.

Como todas las cosas,
con el revés a cuestas,
con el lado olvidado,
con el signo hacia nadie,
el signo naturalmente signo
que sin embargo sirve para todos,
con el signo que tú recuperaste
para velar también la vida, aunque se muera
(tal vez precisamente porque muere),
para velar tu eternidad resucitada
entre aquellos trabajos que emprendías:
unto a ciegas en luz mis calcetines/
y de cada hora mía retoña una distancia/
éste es mi brazo
que por su cuenta rehusó ser ala/
y subo hasta mis pies desde mi estrella.

Murió tu eternidad y la velaste.
Volvió a nacer tu eternidad
y la velamos.
Ahora podemos repetir contigo:
Dios mío, prenderás todas tus velas,
y jugaremos con el viejo dado.

(para César Vallejo)

But the place I know
in this world, nothing less,
becomes manned by reverses.

Like everything,
with the reverse on one's back,
with the forgotten aside,
with the sign toward nobody,
the sign naturally sign
which nonetheless serves for all,
with the sign you restored
to hold a wake for life also, in spite of its death
(perhaps exactly because it dies),
to hold a wake for your eternity revived
among those works you attempted:
I anoint my socks blinded by light/
and from each of my hours sprouts a distance/
this is my arm
that on its own account refused to be wing/
and from my star I climb up to my feet.

Your eternity died and you held its wake.
Your eternity was born again
and we keep a wake over it.
Now we can repeat with you:
My god, you will light all your candles
and we will play with the old dice.

(For César Vallejo)

Undécima.II.25

Cada poema hace olvidar al anterior,
borra la historia de todos los poemas,
borra su propria historia
y hasta borra la historia del hombre
para ganar un rostro de palabras
que el abismo no borre.

También cada palabra del poema
hace olvidar a la anterior,
se desafilia un momento
del tronco multiforme del lenguaje
y después se reencuentra con las otras palabras
para cumplir el rito imprescindible
de inaugurar otro lenguaje.

Y también cada silencio del poema
hace olvidar al anterior,
entre en la gran amnesia del poema
y va envolviendo palabra por palabra,
hasta salir después y envolver el poema
como una capa protectora
que lo preserva de los otros decires.

Todo esto no es raro.
En el fondo,
también cada hombre hace olvidar al anterior,
hace olvidar a todos los hombres.

Si nada se repite igual,
todas las cosas son últimas cosas.
Si nada se repite igual,
todas las cosas son también las primeras.

(en la memoria unitiva de Antonio Porchia)

Eleventh.II.25

Each poem makes us forget the previous one,
erases the history of all poems,
erases its own history
and even erases the history of man
to achieve a countenance of words
the abyss won't erase.

Also each word of the poem
makes us forget the previous word,
disconnects a moment
from the multiform trunk of language
and afterwards re-encounters other words
to complete the necessary rite
of inaugurating another language.

And also each silence of the poem
makes us forget the previous one
in the great amnesia of the poem
and goes on wrapping word by word,
until it emerges afterwards and wraps the poem
like a protective cloak
that preserves it from any other utterance.

This isn't strange.
Deep down,
each man also makes us forget the previous one,
makes us forget all other men.

If nothing is twice the same,
then all things are final.
If nothing is twice the same,
all things are first things.

(To the unifying memory of Antonio Porchia)

Undécima.III.8

Las palabras no son talismanes.
Pero cualquier cosa puede
transmutarse en poesía
si la toca la palabra indicada.

No es asunto de magia ni de alquimia.
Se trata de pensar de otro modo las cosas,
palparlas de otro modo,
abandonar las palabras que las usan
y acudir a las palabras que las cantan,
las palabras que las levantan el el viento
como clavos ardiendo en el asombro.

Estacas convertidas en estrellas,
zapatos para calzar crucifixiones,
cegueras abiertas en la espalda del día,
visiones reservadas para volver a despertar,
ternuras que se postergan para salvar el amor.

Se trata solamente de crear otra voz:
la voz ausente adentro de las cosas.

Eleventh.III.8

Words aren't talismans.
But anything can
transmute itself into poetry
if the right word touches it.

It's not a matter of magic or alchemy.
It's a matter of thinking about things in another way,
touching them differently,
abandoning words that use things,
and turning to words that sing things,
words that lift things up in the wind
like nails burning with surprise.

Stakes turned into stars,
shoes to shoe crucifixions,
open blindness on the shoulder of the day,
visions reserved for reawakening,
tenderness put off to save love.

It's only a question of creating another voice:
the absent voice inside things.

Undécima.IV.2

Los ojos dormidos buscan otro color.
Alguien apagó los colores
como quien apaga las lámparas.
El territorio de los ojos
se convirtió en desierto.

Despertar debiera ser
despertar hacia adentro
y encontrar en el fondo
ese nuevo atributo,
tal vez el duplicado de reserva
de todos los colores.

O quizá la identidad insólita
del que puede encenderlos de nuevo,
como quien enciende las lámparas,
aunque a veces las cubra.

Sin embargo, las lámparas
también se encienden solas.
Tal vez sea eso lo que buscan
los ojos que se duermen.

(para W.S. Merwin)

94

Eleventh.IV.2

Eyes asleep look for another color.
Someone turned off the colors
the way we turn out the light.
The territory of the eyes
turned into a desert.

Waking ought to be
waking toward the inner
and finding in the depth
that new attribute,
perhaps the duplicate in reserve
of all colors.

Or perhaps the unexpected identity
of what could light us up again,
the way we turn on lights,
even though at times we shade them.

Nonetheless, the lamps' light
also comes on all by itself.
Perhaps this is what the eyes that sleep
are seeking.

(For W.S. Merwin)

Undécima.IV.8

Lastimé una mariposa
durante un sueño.
Y no sé ahora cómo hacer
para no soñarla de nuevo.

Otra mariposa
se me acercó despierto:
era la misma mariposa.

Tal vez un pacto
entre el sueño y la viglia
me impida en adelante
reconocer otra.

O mutilado por un sueño
ya sólo puedo ver
esa única mariposa.

Eleventh.IV.8

I injured a butterfly
in a dream.
And now I don't know what to do
to keep from dreaming about it again.

Another butterfly
came close to me while I was awake:
it was the same butterfly.

Perhaps a pact
between dreaming and waking will keep me
from recognizing
any other butterfly in the future.

Or mutilated by a dream now
I can only see
that single butterfly.

Undécima.IV.14

Todo pozo es una entrada al abismo.
No importa que tenga fondo
o aparente tenerlo:
un pozo es siempre la apertura a lo sin fondo.

Espacio para caer o para hundir,
textura diferente del espacio,
tiene el pozo una connivencia
secreta con el hombre.

Y aunque se so rellene,
aunque se plante en él un árbol
o se affirme un cimiento,
todo pozo resulta irrevocable:
su corregido espacio
no será nunca el mismo.

¿No será acaso un pozo
el fundamento de todo?

¿No será todo un pozo?

Eleventh.IV.14

Every well is an entrance into the abyss.
It doesn't matter whether it has a bottom
or seems to have one:
a well is always the opening to the bottomless.

Space in which to fall or to sink,
a different texture of space,
the well has a secret agreement
with man.

And even though it is filled in,
even though a tree is planted in it
or it's cemented up
every well turns out to be unchangeable:
its corrected space
will never be the same.

Isn't a well perhaps
the foundation of everything?

Isn't a well everything?

Undécima.IV.20

La inocencia del niño es una metáfora.
Los ojos no debieron abrirse aquí.
Las primeras miradas son por eso la imagen
de un pájaro que vuela en otro aire.

Abrir los ojos es como empezar a cerrarlos.
Parece que se abandonara una visión
que era más luz que la luz
más claridad que luz,
más levedad abierta.

Pero algo no se resigna a la pérdida
y los ojos conservan por un tiempo
el reflejo de ver,
la costumbre del origen,
el no peso esencial,
la ingravidez que les correspondía.
Y por un breve lapso
mirarán como si vieran.

Después comenzará la otra metáfora:
mirar como si no se viera.

Sólo mucho más tarde,
más allá de las metáforas,
¿tal vez será posible
mirar y ver?

(para Eduardo Acevedo)

Eleventh.IV.20

The innocence of the child is a metaphor.
Eyes shouldn't have opened here.
The first glances are therefore the image
of a bird that flies in another air.

Opening the eyes is like beginning to close them.
It seems a vision has been abandoned
that was more light than light,
clearer than light,
a more open levity.

But something isn't resigned to the loss
and eyes conserve for a time
the reflection of seeing,
the custom of their origin,
their essential weightlessness,
the lack of gravity that is their nature.
And for a brief lapse
they will look as though they see.

Afterwards the other metaphor will begin:
looking as if one doesn't see.

Only much later,
beyond metaphor,
perhaps it will be possible
to look and to see?

(For Eduardo Acevedo)

Undécima.IV.22

Hay que cavar las fuentes.

Hay que cavar las fuentes
y hallar las que están debajo.
Hay que cavar cada paso
y después la huella de cada paso.
Hay que cavar cada palabra
y la auscencia que arrastra cada palabra.
Hay que cavar cada sueño
como si fuera un continente oblicuo.
Hay que cavar el mundo
hasta que sea una sola excavación.

Hay que descubrir las fuentes
que fueron enterradas hace mucho,
tal vez desde el principio.

Hay que iniciar una nueva arqueología:
la arqueología de las fuentes,
la arqueología total.

Eleventh.IV.22

You have to dig up the sources.

You have to dig up the sources
and find what is underneath.
You have to dig up each step
and afterwards the trace of each step.
You have to dig up each word
and the absence that each word brings.
You have to dig up each dream
as if it were an oblique continent.
You have to dig up the world
until it's a single excavation.

You have to discover the sources
that were filled in long ago,
perhaps from the beginning.

You have to initiate a new archeology;
the archeology of sources,
total archeology.

Undécima.IV.23

En todos los caminos hay un hombre
que repite la historia de la noche.
Su vestimenta huele a animal humedecido.
Los viajeros que lo cruzan
miran hacia otra parte
y tratan de no escuchar su murmullo.

Sin embargo,
los pasos de ese hombre no agravian al camino,
porque hace mucho han renunciado a sus huellas.
Sus noctívagos ojos no crucifican las cosas:
se confiesan con ellas.
Sus brazos no son aspas de molino:
el viento se detiene entre sus manos.

Observando con cuidado,
puede verse que ese hombre siembra luz en el camino.
Sin embargo, todos lo abandonan.
No podemos tolerar que la sombra
pueda ser el origen de la luz.

Eleventh.IV.23

On every road there is a man
who repeats the story of the night.
His clothing smells of damp animals.
The travellers who pass
look away
and try not to listen to his muttering.

Nevertheless,
the steps of this man don't harm the road,
because these steps long ago renounced their tracks.
His night-wandering eyes don't crucify things:
but confide in them.
His arms aren't the blades of the windmill:
the wind stops in his hands.

Looking at him carefully,
one can see that this man sows light on the road.
Nevertheless, everyone abandons him.
We cannot stand it that his shadow
might be the source of light.

Undécima.IV.45

Toda palabra es una duda,
todo silencio es otra duda.
Sin embargo,
el enlace de ambas
nos permite respirar.

Todo dormir es un hundimiento,
todo despertar es otro hundimiento.
Sin embargo,
el enlace de ambos
nos permite levantarnos otra vez.

Toda vida es una forma de desvanecerse,
toda muerte es otra forma.
Sin embargo,
el enlace de ambas
nos permite ser un signo en el vacío.

Eleventh.IV.45

Every word is a doubt,
every silence another doubt.
However,
the intertwining of both
lets us breathe.

All sleeping is a sinking down,
all waking another sinking.
However,
the intertwining of both
lets us rise up again.

All life is a form of vanishing,
all death another form.
However,
the intertwining of both
lets us be a sign in the void.

Vertical Poetry:
Recent Poems

Part V

(Unpublished Poems)

Inédito

El número uno me consuela de los demás números.
Un ser humano me consuela de los otros seres humanos.
Una vida me consuela de todas las vidas,
posibles e imposibles.

Haber visto una vez la luz
es como si la hubiera visto siempre.
Haber visto una sola vez la luz
me consuela de no volver a verla nunca.

Un amor me consuela de todos los amores
que tuve y que no tuve.
Una mano me consuela de todas las manos
y hasta un perro me consuela de todos los perros.

Pero tengo un temor:
que mañana llegue a consolarme
más el cero que el uno.

Uncollected

The number one consoles me for the rest of the numbers.
A human being consoles me for other human beings.
A life consoles me for all other lives,
possible and impossible.

To have seen the light once
is as if I had seen it forever.
To have seen the light a single time
consoles me for not ever seeing it again.

One love consoles me for all the loves
I've had and haven't had.
One hand consoles me for all hands
and even a dog consoles me for all dogs.

But I have a fear:
tomorrow to console me
what may arrive
is zero and not one.

Inédito

A veces parece
que estamos en el centro de la fiesta.
Sin embargo
en el centro de la fiesta no hay nadie.
En el centro de la fiesta está el vacío.

Pero en el centro del vacío hay otra fiesta.

Uncollected

Sometimes it seems
as if we are the center of the party.
However
there's nobody at the center of that party.
At that party's center there is emptiness.

But in the center of the emptiness there's another party.

Index of First Lines of Translation

About the Translator

Mary Crow has published three books of translation and three books of poetry. In translation, besides *Vertical Poetry: Recent Poems*, she has published *From the Country of Nevermore: Selected poems of Jorge Teillier* (Wesleyan University Press, 1990) and *Women Who Has Sprouted Wings: Poems by Contemporary Latin American Women Poets* (Latin American Literary Review Press, 1987) which won a Translation Award from Columbia University's Translation Center. She is currently completing two books of poetry in translation: *Sketches Torn From Insomnia* by Olga Orozco and *Ahumada Mall* by Enrique Lihn.

In addition, she has translated a number of other Latin American poets, including Alfonsina Storni, Diana Bellessi, Francisco Madariaga, and Alberto Girri (Argentina), Circe Maia and Idea Vilariño (Uruguay), Marco Martos, Javier Sologuren, and Cecilia Bustamante (Peru), María Mercedes Carranza and Anabel Torres (Colombia), Carmen Orrego and Enrique Gomez-Correa (Chile). Her translations have appeared in such magazines as *American Poetry Review, American Voice, Agni, Sonora Review, Massachusetts Review, The Literary Review, Denver Quarterly, New Orleans Review, Mundus Artium*, and *The Review: Latin American Art and Literature*. In 1982 she received a Fulbright Research Award to study the Surrealist poetry of Peru and Chile. Since then she has returned regularly to Latin America with travel grants from Colorado State University. In 1991 she served on the National Endowment for the Arts' Panel for Translation Fellowships. In the spring of 1992 she will travel to Argentina and Venezuela on a Fulbright Research Award.

David Ignatow wrote the introduction to her collection of poems, *Borders*, which was published in 1989 by Boa editions, Ltd. Her earlier collections were the chapbooks *Going Home* (Lynx House, 1979) and *The Business of Literature* (Four Zoas, 1981). Her poems have appeared in a dozen anthologies, most recently in *The Forgotten Language: Contemporary American Poets on Nature* and *The New Geography of Poetry*, as well as in more than a hundred literary magazines, including *American Poetry Review, Southern Poetry Review, Ploughshares, Prairie Schooner, Northwest Review, North American Review, Poetry East, Graham House Review, Massachusetts Review, New Letters, The River Styx*, and *The Madison Review*. In

116

1984 Crow won a Poetry Fellowship from the National Endowment for the Arts and in 1988 she toured Yugoslavia giving poetry readings and lectures on a Fulbright Creative Writing Award.

Crow is an educator as well as a translator and poet. In 1990 she served on the National Endowment for the Humanities' Panel for Younger Scholar Awards. After serving for the past three years as the Director of Creative Writing, she is currently teaching creative writing at Colorado State University and she also serves as Translation Editor for *Colorado Review*.

Printed in the USA
CPSIA information can be obtained
at www.ICGtesting.com
JSHW082220140824
68134JS00015B/641